ENTERTAINMENT ROOMS
THEATERS, BARS, & GAME ROOMS

Tina Skinner

4880 Lower Valley Road, Atglen, Pennsylvania 19310

ACKNOWLEDGMENTS

Special thanks to the many contributors to this book, most specially Laura Elder, who added a lot of the awesome impression these pages pack. Ginger Doyle worked tirelessly to compile, organize, and communicate, and this book would not have come together without her assistance. As you look through these images it is important to acknowledge the true talent and vision behind every design, and that the art of capturing that vision in still-life form is owing to the many talented photographers whose work is featured here-in. Whenever possible, they have been credited and contact info listed in the back of the book to help them earn future commissions. Finally, thanks to you, dear reader, for purchasing a book. Books are precious, time-honored resources, and need our continued support.

Schiffer Books are available at special discounts for bulk purchases for sales promotions or premiums. Special editions, including personalized covers, corporate imprints, and excerpts can be created in large quantities for special needs. For more information contact the publisher:

Published by Schiffer Publishing Ltd.
4880 Lower Valley Road
Atglen, PA 19310
Phone: (610) 593-1777; Fax: (610) 593-2002
E-mail: Info@schifferbooks.com

For the largest selection of fine reference books on this and related subjects, please visit our web site at
www.schifferbooks.com
We are always looking for people to write books on new and related subjects. If you have an idea for a book please contact us at the above address.

This book may be purchased from the publisher.
Include $5.00 for shipping.
Please try your bookstore first.
You may write for a free catalog.

In Europe, Schiffer books are distributed by
Bushwood Books
6 Marksbury Ave.
Kew Gardens
Surrey TW9 4JF England
Phone: 44 (0) 20 8392 8585; Fax: 44 (0) 20 8392 9876
E-mail: info@bushwoodbooks.co.uk
Website: www.bushwoodbooks.co.uk

Copyright © 2010 by Schiffer Publishing, Ltd.

Library of Congress Control Number: 2009941991

Designed by Mark David Bowyer
Type set in Trajan Pro / Korinna BT

ISBN: 978-0-7643-3407-8
Printed in China

CONTENTS

Introduction 4

Rooms That Convert 5

Home Theaters 14

    The Dedicated Room 14

    Super Dramatic Cinematic 43

    Full Cinema Experiences 78

    Dinner Theater 90

The Corner Bar............................. 96

Sports Bars & Game Rooms 120

Wine Cellars............................... 146

Ending with a Splash 153

Contributors............................. 157

Photographers........................... 159

INTRODUCTION

Fantasy has become reality in the lives of many homeowners. In a few generations, we've evolved from the miracle of moving pictures shown to audiences accompanied by a local pianist, to color television, to affordable projectors and big screens in our homes. In some cases, multiple screens replicate the visual smorgasbord of simultaneous sports broadcasts. "Extra" rooms in our homes are insulated to create the soundproof experience or, perhaps, the perfect temperature and humidity for a vast collection of aging wines. Cocktail hour with friends happens around corner bars or in entire rooms outfitted in custom cabinetry, with all the top rail spirits, and the luxury of space to accommodate pool tables.

This book is a wonderful tour of the extravagances now within reach of the middle class homeowner, packed with ideas to help you plan your own home paradise. Imagine what you'll save on travel after investing in your own home vacation plan. The only obstacle is working out time-sharing issues with the spouse and children!

My own fascination is the potential these rooms have for unlocking creativity. Once we step beyond the time-honored ideas of kitchens, living rooms, and guest powder rooms and the necessity of presenting the proper, conservative, beige-white facade, we enter into these alternative rooms, where personalities really start to present themselves. Once the budget of rooms has extended to the point where they are being created solely for pleasure, it becomes a matter of pure fantasy. Herein, I believe, the true joy and exuberance of nesting can be expressed and the individual can shine through. By experiencing others' freedom of expression, I hope you can unleash your own and allow yourself to express your love of history, your excitement about the future, or your fascination with the exotic. The options are endless...

ROOMS THAT CONVERT

A projector on the back wall fills the big-screen at the front of this living room/theater. The other components of this magic fill a bank of appliances that control this custom electronic paradise.
Courtesy of Modern Home Systems

For the modest budget, these rooms illustrate ways in which the most comfortable room in the home can become the home theater, too. Living rooms may or may not advertise their occupation by a big screen and a projector. Many convert with the flick of a switch, while others were designed with new cabinetry that frames the prominent screen. Following are a few worthy ideas.

A theater experience was built into a large, open floor plan. Shelves and an angled wall concentrate the sound and focus for movie time. *Courtesy of Winn Wittman Architecture*

Photographer David Beightol

Horseshoe seating emphasizes a democratic approach to enjoying the big screen, in a spacious rec room with fireside seating and billiards all part of the mix. *Courtesy of Connected Technologies*

A control panel is the behind the magic that takes place when a penthouse room transforms to home theater. The surprise is a screen that rises from a granite countertop, then tucks away to preserve a precious view. *Courtesy of Modern Home Systems*

Photographer Jim Brady

A lofty getaway is naturally sound-proofed by thick log walls. A projector benefits from the high ceiling, filling a big screen that takes advantage of space created by rafters. *Courtesy of Strongwood Log Home Company*

Photographer Joe Hilliard from Hilliard Photography

Note: Continued on the next two pages.

Photographer Dustin Peck Photography

A sunny wall with French doors, sidelights, transoms, and two big windows is quickly transformed by light-blocking shades, followed by a drop-down screen. *Courtesy of Audio Video One, Inc.*

HOME THEATERS

T he next step in home entertainment, and one of the biggest trends, is the investment in a home theater. With technology becoming more afford-able, an entire industry has grown up around transforming a spare room, basement, or garage into a home theater venue. As you'll see, the investment is resulting in rooms that range from comfortable seating with a big screen, to huge rooms packed with imaginative decor and outfitted to host large audiences. Our presentation follows this progression, from rooms dedicated solely to the viewing experience, to rooms that express themselves in fantas-tically conceived decor, to those that virtually recreate a theater, with lobbies and silver screen-era decor.

THE DEDICATED ROOM

Today's technology allows homeowners to bring all the excitement and impact of the theater experience to a dedicated room in their home. Soundproofing isolates the experience, while technology presents projection units, retractable screens, fiber-optic lighting, surround sound, and many other bells and whistles within afford-able reach.

Photos: www.digimaxstudios.com

A control panel makes the theater experience possible. Behind it, the complicated mechan-ics of coordinating electronic instruments is illustrated. For the owners and their guests, though, it's all about the big screen, comfy seats, and the gentle, star-like fiber optic lighting from above. *Courtesy of Sights – N – Sounds*

Photographer Jeff Vyain

Carpeting and sound panels add to the insulated atmosphere conducive to the total suspension of reality.
Courtesy of Digitech Custom

Photographer Jeff Vyain

Red wall panels add a lush, dark atmosphere to this theater experience, illuminated by sconces.
Courtesy of Digitech Custom

Photographer Dustin Peck Photography

Fiber optics make the stars twinkle overhead while the Hollywood stars work their magic on screen.
Courtesy of Audio Video One, Inc.

Drapes draw back for a theater experience framed by clean Art Deco lines that recall Hollywood's classic era. *Courtesy of A Plus Electronics*

Photographer Henry Nelson, Wichita, Kansas

Photographer Henry Nelson, Wichita, Kansas

Faux painting on one wall increases the sense of scale in this already spacious ten-seat venue. The stone-like backdrop for the screen is carried forward in pillared frames that evoke a Romanesque experience. *Courtesy of A Plus Electronics*

Ever feel chilly in an air-conditioned theater? Provisions have been provided for just such an event in this stay-at-home cinema. An arts-and-crafts era border creates a rustic crown molding between rich wood columns. A love seat in back honors the pursuit of the newly-in-love to snuggle during great movies. *Courtesy of Audio Video One, Inc.*

Photographer Dustin Peck Photography

Photographer Henry Nelson, Wichita, Kansas

Rustic doors and brown suede ground this theater in a comfortable, country aesthetic.
Courtesy of A Plus Electronics

A theater room draws family members from an adjacent sunny room to comfy chairs for big screen entertainment. Footlights on the raised platform guide the feet of those who step out for a popcorn refill. *Courtesy of Golden Eagle Log Homes*

Photographer Angie Seckinger

An attic space gets a makeover as a home theater. The bar seating in the back is desirable with the big screen.
Courtesy of Diane Gordy Interiors

Wood tones and golden walls keep the feeling of home comfort
in a domestic theater venue. *Courtesy of Modern Home Systems*

Photographer Jim Brady

Photographer Strawbridge Photo

Five screens cater to the ADD personality, mesmerizing with a wall of action.
Courtesy of MPM Interiors

This converted Exercise Room functions perfectly as a media room with its wood panel walls and multi-level floor offering prime viewing from several sitting areas.
Courtesy of James D. LaRue Architects

Photographer www.ColesHairston.com

Photographer David Beightol

Handsome wood paneling frames a spacious screen and the bank of speakers below.
Courtesy of Connected Technologies

A faux finish gives a metallic appeal to a barrel vault ceiling in this home screening room.
Courtesy of Vanguard Studios

Photographer William Horlacher, IV

Comfort was a primary consideration in the design of this home screening room. From comfy seats each outfitted with pillows and blankets, to a big selection of snacks and beverages, the owners set out to make sure that guests would enjoy their theater experience. Soundboards help insulate the walls, and fitted screens block the outside world for the duration. A wall panel next to the screen reveals the mechanics of the experience. *Courtesy of Audio Video One, Inc.*

Photographer David Beightol

Modular furniture allows family and friends to mix up the arrangement. An extensive movie collection fills the library adjacent to the control panel. *Courtesy of Connected Technologies*

A faux finish gives these walls a leather look, paired with green velvet curtains in classic cinema style.
Courtesy of Connected Technologies

Photographer David Beightol

Photographer David Beightol

Extra pillows on the floor underline the point of a home theater – this
is home. You can curl up on the floor if you want. It's clean and casual.
Courtesy of Connected Technologies

Photographer David Beightol

Wood paneling and curtains conceal the mechanics of a home theater. The stage was made deep enough to be useful should friends or family members dare to put on their own show or recital. *Courtesy of Connected Technologies*

Photographer Strawbridge Photo

Plush velvet seating cushions the home theater experience. An inset shows
the view toward the wall-sized screen. *Courtesy of MPM Interiors*

"Skylights" open and close on this rich, warmly furnished home theater venue, and offer the homeowners the option of putting on a light show or revealing the stars at any time of day or night. *Courtesy of First Impressions Theme Theatres*

Photographer Barry Grossman, Grossman Photography

Photographer David Beightol

Ironwork caps the half walls that back three tiers of seating descending toward the screen. Speakers underline the screen and fill the base of the columns flanking it. *Courtesy of Connected Technologies*

SUPER DRAMATIC CINEMATIC

Arguably, there was a pretty thin line in deciding that these theaters represented "over the top" vs. any others presented. Just the idea of having a home theater is so far beyond the dreams of our grandparents. Still, you may find that the following facilities manage to evoke a sense of wow in an ever increasing level of expectations.

Photographer Marisa Pellegrini Photography

Rich textiles cocoon this private theater in opulence. The golden tones of a leopard print carpet are picked up in a compass star medallion on the ceiling, while burgundy and lavender hues lend themselves to the over-the-top eye-candy that characterizes Hollywood productions. *Courtesy of Interior Designs, Inc.*

Photographer Barry Grossman, Grossman Photography

A passion for sports drove the design of this home theater, along with a whimsical red-white-and-blue patriotism that celebrates the American movie experience. Multiple screens keep the action racing. *Courtesy of First Impressions Theme Theatres*

Earthy tones evoke an elegant Mission-style, and mohair seating gives everyone an ideal view of the big screen. An impressive light show is revealed through an elegant drop ceiling of wood. The inset picture reveals the corner bar for libations. *Courtesy of First Impressions Theme Theatres*

Photographer Randy Cordero, Cordero Studios

A hallway outside this screening room has refreshments and posters to advertise upcoming attractions. Seven seats preserve a sense of intimacy within a confined area flanked by speakers poised to rock the walls. Inset images reveal the popcorn stand and the even more impressive electronics panel. *Courtesy of First Impressions Theme Theatres*

Photographer Barry Grossman, Grossman Photography

A wild-west theme delights the master of the house. A cowpoke is framed above footlights for the fifty-cent tour, while the curtain rises all the way for screenings of beloved westerns.
Courtesy of First Impressions Theme Theatres

Photographer Barry Grossman, Grossman Photography

An exotic Indian atmosphere brings the opulence
of a Maharaja's palace to the home theater, with
pillows and sofas providing an invitation to enjoy
the cinematic experience in a supine position.
Courtesy of First Impressions Theme Theatres

Photographer Barry Grossman, Grossman Photography

As a "convertible theatre" this cinema becomes a guest suite in five minutes, thanks to reclining seats. A sound proof room was needed in the condominium conversion, making the space all the more desirable for an overnight visitor.
Courtesy of First Impressions Theme Theatres

Photographer Z

Slate blues and rich cordovan create a contrast of warm and cool in this spacious home theater. The decor also strikes a balance between classic architectural detail like warm chestnut wood panels, and acute and curvilinear shapes to house the very latest technology. *Courtesy of First Impressions Theme Theatres*

Photographer Jerry Blow Architectural Photography

Louis XIV would have felt at home in this theater, before the projector kicked in. Wall boxes conceal speakers for surround sound brilliance, and the monogrammed screen surround frames a full twelve feet of visual feast. Ten thickly upholstered and fringed CinePalaisLounger™ chairs front a granite bar, where there's another level of seating. An inset image shows the rouge entry to this French-style film experience.
Courtesy of First Impressions Theme Theatres

Photographer CK Architectural Photography

Recliners offer friends and family a chance to kick back in blue velvet.
A mini-kitchen beyond makes it possible to prolong the movie-going
experience indefinitely. *Courtesy of First Impressions Theme Theatres*

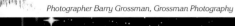

Photographer Barry Grossman, Grossman Photography

Crimson and gold color accents this Mahogany-paneled home theater, lit from above by flickering stars.
Courtesy of First Impressions Theme Theatres

Photographer Barry Grossman, Grossman Photography

Comfort was foremost in the creation of this
fourteen-seat show venue. Those up front can
literally kick back on power-driven lounge chairs.
Courtesy of First Impressions Theme Theatres

Photographer Barry Grossman, Grossman Photography

No one feels crowded in this spacious theater where nine primo motorized chairs offer uninterrupted stadium-style views of the big screen. Insets show the entryway to the space, as well as the screen with the elaborately draped Austrian curtain drawn.
Courtesy of First Impressions Theme Theatres

Photographer Barry Grossman, Grossman Photography

A semi-circular seating arrangement puts everyone up-close and personal with the big screen, while surrounding them in opulence. Besides gilded paneling worthy of a Roman emperor, the room also includes an elevated ceiling illuminated by fiber optic stars. *Courtesy of First Impressions Theme Theatres*

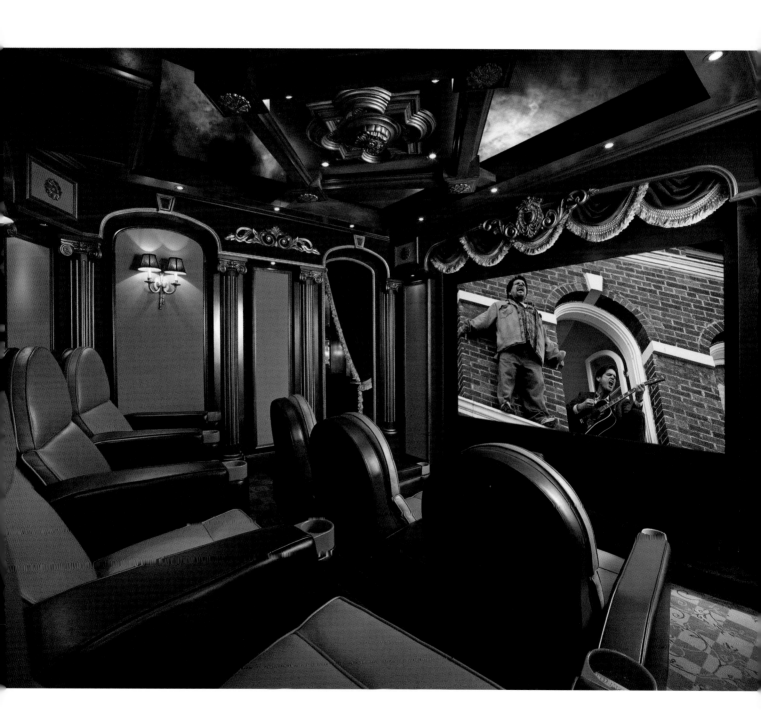

Photographer Barry Grossman, Grossman Photography

Lavish layers of wood molding and ornamentation create the Neo-classic appeal of this theater, impeccably tailored in an interplay of stripes and checks. The inset image shows the columned entry to this household retreat.
Courtesy of First Impressions Theme Theatres

Photographer Barry Grossman, Grossman Photography

An Asian theme brings exoticism and excitement to this spacious theater retreat, with a dragon that has flashing fiber-optic eyes and spews fake fire. *Courtesy of First Impressions Theme Theatres*

Photographer Jerry Blow Architectural Photography

Every seat in a winner in a home theater built on a floating riser floor. Enough headroom was left over to allow for a special drop ceiling with faux sky beyond. *Courtesy of First Impressions Theme Theatres*

Photographer Randall Cordero, Cordero Studios

The opulence of this home theater might delay the start of the movie, as guests try to take it all in. An inset photo illustrates the big screen before the curtains are drawn. *Courtesy of First Impressions Theme Theatres*

Photographer CK Architectural Photography

A keyboard adds another purpose to this theater room, where the homeowner jams with friends. *Courtesy of First Impressions Theme Theatres*

FULL CINEMA EXPERIENCES

From their full lobbies with ticket booths and snack bars, to their elaborate interiors, these home theaters recreate the going-out experience, even if you only just walked downstairs. The effect launches you into the suspension of disbelief and heightens the "movie going" adventure.

Photographer Stephen Paul Whitsitt

A black and gold color scheme unites lobby with theater interior for an experience straight out of film's golden era. Popcorn and candy kiosks adorn the "lobby" and velvet ropes hold back the crowds. It's never crowded, though, with comfy seating for seven, and aisles where more chairs can be brought in without violating the fire marshal's code. *Courtesy of Interior Dezign by 2 of a Kind*

Note: Continued on the next four pages.

Photographer Stephen Paul Whitsitt

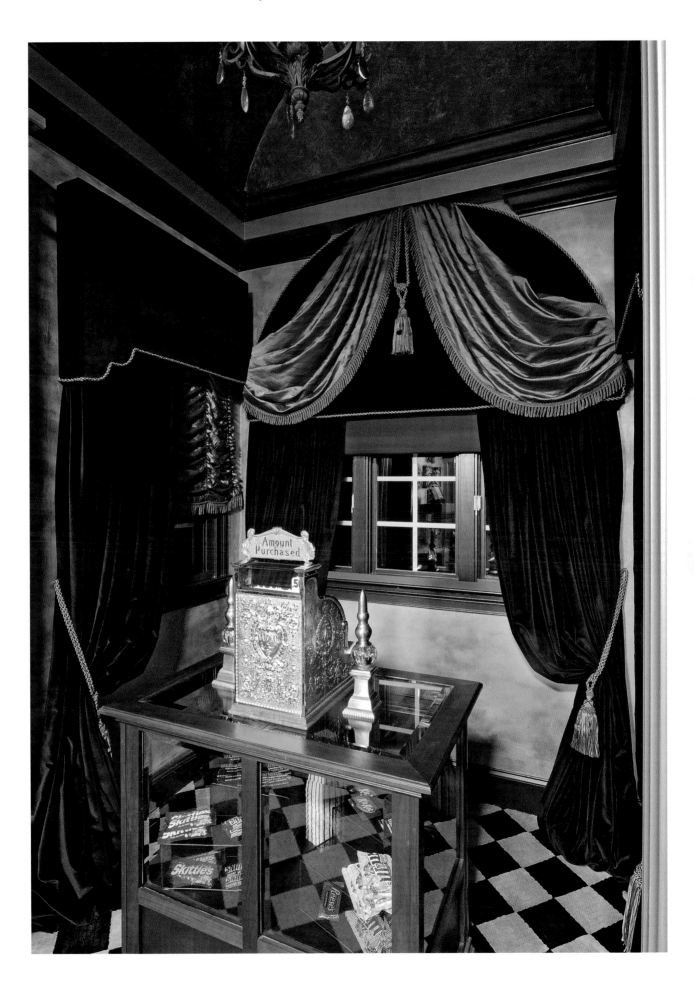

Photographer Stephen Paul Whitsitt

Three rows of primo seating descend a home theater, passing down a row of Corinthian columns, under star-lit domed ceilings. *Courtesy of First Impressions Theme Theatres*

Photographer Ron Shefer

Photographer Keith Rocke

This elaborate lobby, with a full-scale, fully-stocked, snack bar and an actual ticket booth, is a prelude to an enormous palatial residential cinema experience. Within this home theater there is luxury seating for up to twenty-eight friends and family members.
Courtesy of First Impressions Theme Theatres

Photographer Z

Here's an incredible home theater – the whole thing. An outdoor facade creates an architectural impression against an illuminated night sky. Within, a plush red interior seats an intimate party around a stage shaped like a film reel. Actually, this theater is part of an incredible faux city block of buildings, each containing a different room. Note the special lounge chair up front for a beloved dog. His story is interesting – he wandered into the owner's driveway, sick and starving. His rescuer made him part of the action, with his own cushioned viewing platform right up front, and his own "popcorn" bowl for screening events. *Courtesy of First Impressions Theme Theatres*

Photographer Dan Forer

Neon-lights usher guests through an entrance and lobby designed to impress, providing the homeowners the ability to give the full-theater experience to their friends. Within the spacious theater, where twenty-seven are comfortably seated, a ceiling medallion conceals the projector, while revealing the Art Deco inspiration that adorned many theaters during the height of the silver screen era. *Courtesy of First Impressions Theme Theatres*

Photographer Barry Grossman, Grossman Photography

Even before the movie starts rolling, you've entered another dimension in this home theater. Lighting effects and fantasy features put you in the captain's chair for an out-of-this-world experience. An inset photo gives a glimpse into the lobby, where treats are on tap. *Courtesy of First Impressions Theme Theatres*

DINNER THEATER

Here are some ideas for home theaters that incorporate bars and food preparation areas, as well as handsome surfaces upon which to serve. If you're hoping to host dinner theater experiences, these designs may be right for you.

Photographer William Horlacher, IV

Four seats attest to the privilege of inclusion in this theater experience. The spacious room is handsomely framed in molded woodwork and classic arches. The action on screen can be seen both fore and aft, so those at the bar have a choice of directions atop their stools. *Courtesy of Audio Video One, Inc.*

Photographer Dustin Peck Photography

Intermissions are anticipated, even during the most exciting screening, with the bar so close at hand. Besides making the master of the house the host with the most, the bar closets the digital heart of this cozy, wood-paneled cinema. *Courtesy of Audio Video One, Inc.*

Durable enough for a kids' movie night and sophisticated enough for an adult soiree, this media room remains an ever handsome and gracious host.
Courtesy of Howarth Designs LLC

THE CORNER BAR

A dedicated bar has always topped the interior furnishings wish list for those who like to imbibe with friends. The amenity is realizing new scale in today's home plans. We start out small in this chapter, but as you can see, the "don't drink and drive" movement has added new dimension to the ambitions of home bars.

Photographer Jacqueline Epstein

A bar nook and seating area uplift this room even before the spirits are poured. Glass mosaics, stainless steel, granite, and hand-made ceramics add to this festive environment. *Courtesy of Jacqueline's Interior Design Studio, Inc.*

A casual entertainment area creates conversation nooks as well as a lively bar area. The comfy seating area connects with a wine cellar and a home bar stocked with alternative libations.
Courtesy of Trublood Company

Photographer Jacqueline Epstein

In a beautiful sun-room off the family kitchen, a bar serves as a gathering place. *Courtesy of Jacqueline's Interior Design Studio, Inc.*

Photographer Accent Photography

A compact corner has been set up for libations, with spacious wine storage and a seated counter for shared indulgences. *Courtesy of Interiors by Renee & Assoc.*

A corner bar services the waterfront patio or a warm gathering space by the fireplace –
whichever Mother Nature's whims dictate. *Brion Jeannette Architecture*

A backlit bar was designed to showcase the client's choices in spirits, wine, and sound. It also has a built-in beverage and wine fridge. *Courtesy of Scandia Kitchens, Visions Design Center & Charlotte Bogardus*

Photographer Will Hare Photography

A classic bar and billiard room evokes gentlemanly gatherings, crowned by a classic coffered ceiling. *Drion Jeannette Architecture*

Photographer Stephen Paul Whitsitt

A corner bar draws a small crowd, while comfortable seating keeps them close.
Courtesy of Bella Domicile, Inc.

An extensive wet bar area serves the living room beyond, finally moving the party out of the kitchen and toward the more comfortable seating. *Courtesy of Bella Domicile, Inc.*

Photographer Stephen Paul Whitsitt

A cowboy rides into a bar... In this case, anyway, the horse is welcome. Lit from above by a loft overlooking a riding arena beyond, this home bar provides a classic retreat where hunting stories are related following the chase. *Courtesy of Atwood Fine Architectural Cabinetry*

Photographer Charles Meachum

An accomplished athlete can recall past competitions with friends while sitting around this home bar. Trophies and beautiful glassware are displayed in lighted cabinets, while coolers below keep beverages at the ideal temperature. *Courtesy of Stimmel Consulting Group, Inc.*

Photographer Dave Adams Photography

Genuine theater seats usher in the mood and focus all eyes in this retro home theater. Intermission is the best, with a lush lounge area just beyond, and a fully stocked bar.
Courtesy of Reynolds Gualco Architecture – Interior Design

A stage is the perfect format for performances by talented guests and family members, and provides a platform for daily practice. Adjacent, a wet bar is fully stocked with snacks and libations for this lively room. Designer: Stephen Pararo, ASID, IIDA; *Courtesy of Pineapple House Interior Design*

Scott Moore Photography

Photographer Jeff Vyain

A home theater is ceremoniously separated from a larger entertainment area by structural columns, so those sitting at the bar are also connected with what's happening on the big screen. *Courtesy of Digitech Custom*

Bar-front seating brings everyone to the fore for action on the framed screen. *Courtesy of MPM Interiors*

A pub-like room sits off a wine cellar, creating a club-like atmosphere. Rock walls seem to date this charming escape to antiquity. *Courtesy of Valentini's Custom Wine Cellars*

A custom home diner feeds the nostalgia of friends who remember fountain drinks and sock hops. Besides a bar/counter that easily seats eight, plenty of floor space was spared for jitterbug fanatics. *Courtesy of Vanessa DeLeon Associates*

Photographer: Jay Rosenblatt

Photographer Tom Grimes Photography

An elegant wood bar creates a custom-designed gathering space. Note the wine cellar beyond.
Courtesy of Trublood Company

"Life is short, the art long," when design clients agreed to knock down walls and extend their home in order to make room for new entertaining opportunities and to create a warm welcome for family and friends using a Russian Art collection as a focal point. *Courtesy of James Yarosh Associates Fine Art*

Photographer John M. Hall

SPORTS BARS
& GAME ROOMS

Photographer Eric Figge Photography

A subterranean retreat offers libations and friendly competitions. River stone adorns the descending stairs, adding a sense of insulation, while a gilded ceiling augments the illumination. *Brion Jeannette Architecture*

One of the most likely casual social events in the average home is a gathering to watch a big sports match. An entire genre of finger foods and paper plates has evolved from the theme. So why not have a room dedicated to such events? All fun and games, the following rooms are dedicated to camaraderie and a little healthy competition. From pool to poker, there are great ideas on ways to involve guests in the excitement beyond that on the big screens.

Photographer Stephen Paul Whitsitt

This rec room instantly elevated the proud new owners to neighborhood hosts. This expansive hangout is dedicated to social fun, and with all this, why would you ever go out? *Courtesy of Shelly Design Inc.*

Note: Continued on the next two pages.

Photographer Stephen Paul Whitsitt

Photographer Stephen Paul Whitsitt

A wall of historic botanical prints creates the effect of another window in a billiard room. The coffered ceiling defines the space, supporting a chandelier that illuminates the room's central mass. *Courtesy of Design By Shearer*

Pinball, pool, and cool beverages are on tap in this enticing games center. *Courtesy of Northbay Kitchen & Bath*

Photographer Stephen Paul Whitsitt

A harlequin pattern on the floor unites this classic entertainment area, and electrifies it with pattern. Beautiful custom cabinetry, wrought-iron bar stools, and a host of other elements emphasize the importance given to this gathering space for family and close friends. *Courtesy of Interior Dezign by 2 of a Kind*

Note: Continued on the next two pages.

Photographer Stephen Paul Whitsitt

Photographer Stephen Paul Whitsitt

A games room is furnished with a
built-in bar and padded chairs at the rail
upholstered to match the billiard table.
Plaid wallpaper creates a classic pub
effect, paired with custom cabinetry.
Courtesy of Bella Domicile, Inc.

Photographer Bob Marcum

A rustic loft provides a game getaway. *Courtesy of Strongwood Log Home Company*

Photographer Dave Adams Photography

Storage and shelving help keep things orderly in a highly trafficked rec room. In one space, there's computer access, big screen chilling, and a pool table for friendly competition. *Courtesy of Reynolds Gualco Architecture – Interior Design*

Photographer Ken Hild

An enormous fish tank overlooks a bar and billiard room, as well as the living room on the other side. It also acts as a sound buffer when cheering for teams on the multiple screens gets a little out of control. *Courtesy of PYW Interiors*

This fire-warmed billiards room has been decorated for upcoming Christmas festivities.
Courtesy of PYW Interiors

A barrel vault window opening and brick wall add to the sense of escape in a getaway, fun room.
Courtesy of Lasting Impressions Triangle Staging & Design

Photographer Morgan Howarth

Far from the subterranean stereotype, this post-modern "man cave" proves that entertaining can be tasteful and stylish. The wet bar has custom, ebonized quarter sawn oak cabinetry and shelving and Green Hawaii granite on the bar. The art deco style fireplace surround has a green marble hearth and black granite surround.

Photographer: Eugene Parciasepe, Jr.

Sports are celebrated in a room dedicated to game. Transom and sidelight windows add to the airy atmosphere, illuminating a beautiful parquet floor. *Courtesy of Maureen Fiori*

Photographer: John Armich

All kinds of fun are packed into this lofty retreat. Billiards and poker keep friendly gatherings busy, and a model railroad is on hand to fiddle with when everyone goes home. *Courtesy of Linda Daly, ASID, Interior Design*

Photographer Dustin Peck Photography

A sports fan displays a collection of memorabilia and personal trophies above the bar in a guy-oriented game room. Small monitors allow guests to keep up on different games, while a main screen is perfect for feature presentation. *Courtesy of Audio Video One, Inc.*

Photographer Henry Nelson, Wichita, Kansas

Kitchen, dining area, and bar seating all offer premium seating in a theater setting.
Courtesy of A Plus Electronics

The billiard table and game table are outfitted in rich aubergine for a contemporary touch amidst an island-inspired atmosphere of textured walls, slate floors, and woven rattan accents. *Courtesy of Jill Ciccone, JC Design Interiors.*

WINE CELLARS

W ine is the gift you give yourself and, with a wine cellar, a case of wine keeps on giving. For the connoisseur, a wine cellar is the only way to preserve the integrity of a wine as it ages. The possession of such a room offers a big impression, too, and creates a haven where friends can escape to sample a special vintage.

A glass wall preserves the view of beverages as they age in a carefully controlled environment. A tasting table just beyond awaits the grand uncorking. *Courtesy of Valentini's Custom Wine Cellars*

An arch clears space for a countertop where bottles can be labeled for storage or uncorked for pleasure. *Courtesy of Valentini's Custom Wine Cellars*

Hand-chiseled Travertine stone on the floors pairs with ornate cast aluminum and hand-forged wrought iron gates with grape vine details to create a classic framework for a wine cellar. Real California stucco and cultured-stone walls add to the old-world atmosphere. The wood beams simulate hand-hewn pine. The tasting room is connected with the household sound system, making for a seamless transition for host and guests from dinner table upstairs to this secluded space where they can continue the libations.

Spent bottles add brilliance to the wall of a tasting room, while their virgin cousins await their turn in the light in the controlled environment of the wine cellar beyond. Brion Jeannette Architecture / *Courtesy of Germano Wine Cellars*

Photographer Jeff Kroeze Photography

A baronial dining space provides seating next to an amply stocked wine cellar. Vaulted brick
ceilings, stained glass, and richly-carved wood furnishings add to the atmosphere of gentility.
Brion Jeannette Architecture

Photographer Eric Figge Photography

A tasting table serves those hasty to enjoy the treasures in wine cellar beyond.
Brion Jeannette Architecture

ENDING WITH A SPLASH

Photographer Heritage Pools Limited

A deck along the outside wall helps provide a dose of the great outdoors and exposure to a little sun, even on brisk winter days.
Courtesy of Heritage Pools

F inally, here's a dip into a special self-indulgence: an investment in a pool that serves year-round as home retreat. Be warned, though, that you'll become the most popular house on the block when the weather turns chilly and friends and family need a retreat.

Photographer Heritage Pools Limited

An elevated ceiling adds dimension to a pool room with limited gathering space outside the pool. An adjacent spa has a seating edge the helps accommodate additional guests when they are not in the water. *Courtesy of Heritage Pools*

An indoor pool is a perfect excuse for a get together in any weather. Here a small pool room dedicates the maximum amount of space to watery pleasures, with the inside wall of the pool doubling as seating. *Brion Jeannette Architecture*

French doors and windows open to create an indoor/outdoor environment when weather permits.
When it doesn't, the fun goes on. *Courtesy of Heritage Pools*

CONTRIBUTORS

A Plus Electronics
Park City, Kansas
316-265-0366
www.apluselectronics.com

Atwood Fine Architectural
Cabinetry
Greenville, South Carolina
864-233-3730
www.atwoodcabinetry.com

Audio Video One, Inc.
Winston-Salem, North Carolina
336-771-3000
www.avone.net

Bella Domicile, Inc.
Madison, Wisconsin
608-271-8241
www.belladomicile.com

Connected Technologies
Colorado Springs, Colorado
719-598-3933
www.connected-technologies.com

Linda Daly, ASID, Interior Design
Ivyland, Pennsylvania
215-598-3345
www.interioroutlook.com

Vanessa DeLeon Associates
Edgewater, New Jersey
201-224-9060
www.vanessadeleon.com

Design by Schearer
Chapel Hill, North Carolina
919-490-1922

Digitech Custom
Carmel, Indiana
317-580-1922
www.digitechcustom.net

Maureen Fiori, AKBD, Allied Member
ASID
Franklin Lakes, New Jersey
201-835-5051

First Impressions Theme Theatres
Miami, Florida
800-305-7545
www.CineLoungers.com

Germano Custom Wine Cellars
Columbia, Tennessee
615-586-2142
www.germanocustomwinecellars.com

Golden Eagle Log Homes
Wisconsin Rapids, Wisconsin
800-270-5025
www.goldeneagleloghomes.com

Diane Gordy Interiors
Bethesda, Maryland
301-229-9500
www.dianegordy.com

Tom Grimes Photography
Pennington, New Jersey
917-570-1823
www.tomgrimes.com

Heritage Pools Unlimited
Guildford, Surrey, England
01483 235858
www.heritagepools.co.uk

Howarth Designs LLC
Arlington, Virginia
703-671-8448
www.howarthdesigns.com

Interiors by Renee & Assoc.
Raleigh, North Carolina
919-212-3326
www.interiorsbyrenee.com

Interior Dezign by 2 of a Kind
Elon, North Carolina
336-684-5287

Jacqueline's Interior
Design Studio, Inc.
Cherry Hill, New Jersey
856-424-9998

JC Design Interiors
Shrewsbury, New Jersey
732-501-5081

Brion Jeannette Architecture
Newport Beach, California
949-645-5854
www.customarchitecture.com

James D. LaRue Architects
Austin, Texas
512-347-1688
www.larue-architects.com

Lasting Impressions
Triangle Staging & Design
Raleigh, North Carolina
919-324-2225
www.TriangleStaging.com

Modern Home Systems
San Diego, California
858-554-0404
www.modernhomesystems.com

MPM Interiors
Durham, North Carolina
919-593-3369

Northbay Kitchen & Bath
Petaluma, California
707-769-1646
www.4kitchens.com

Pineapple House Interior Design
Atlanta, Georgia
404-897-5551
www.pineapplehouse.com

PYW Interiors
Miller Place, New York
631-209-1500
www.pywinteriors.com

Reynolds Gualco Architecture
– Interior Design
Sacramento, California
916-456-3720
www.rgaid.com

Shelly Design, Inc.
Cincinnati, Ohio
513-752-1606
www.shellydesigninc.com

Sights – N – Sounds
Seaford, New York
516-679-9701
www.hometheater.biz

Stimmel Consulting Group, Inc.
Ambler, Pennsylvania
215-542-0772
www.stimmeldesign.com

Strongwood Log Home Company
Waupaca, Wisconsin
888-989-9299
www.strongwoodloghome.com

Karla Trincanello, Allied Member
ASID
Florham Park, New Jersey
973-765-9013
www.interiordecisions.com

Trueblood Company
Springhouse, Pennsylvania
215-643-6840
www.truebloodco.com

Valentini's Custom Wine Cellars
Chandler, Arizona
888-330-6371
www.valentinis.com

Vanguard Studios, Inc.
Austin, Texas
512-918-8312
www.vanguardstudio.com

Visions Design Center
Dedham, Massachusetts
781-329-0028

Winn Wittman Architecture
Austin, Texas
512-473-3738
www.winnwittman.com

James Yarosh Associates Fine Art
Holmdel, New Jersey
732-539-8859
www.jamesyarosh.com

PHOTOGRAPHERS

Dave Adams Photography
Winters, California
530-795-2529
www.daveadamsphotography.com

John Armich
Alburtis, Pennsylvania
215-262-8015
www.johnarmich.com

Paul Bardagjy
Austin, Texas
512-452-9636
www.bardagjyphoto.com

David Beightol, Beightol Photomedia
719-593-7006
www.beightol.com

Bill Blizzard
Voorhees, New Jersey

Jim Brady
www.jimbradyphoto.com

Bob DiNatale
Medford, Massachusetts
781-219-3831
www.bobdinatale.com

Edie Ellison, Accent Photography
Greenville, South Carolina
864-329-9302
www.waterscapesphotography.com

Eric Figge Photography
www.ericfigge.com

Steve Geraci of Reflex Photos
Bohemia, New York
631-567-8777
www.reflexphoto.com

Tom Grimes Photography
Pennington, New Jersey
917-570-1823
www.tomgrimes.com

Coles Hairston
Austin, Texas
512-416-6060
www.ColesHairston.com

John M. Hall
212-757-0369
www.johnmhallphotographs.com

Will Hare Photography
Orange, California
714-771-2542
www.willharephoto.com

Ken Hild
Shoreham, New York
516-808-2526
web.mac.com/kenhildphotography

Joe Hilliard, Hilliard Photography
574-361-0616

Morgan Howarth
240-377-1766
www.morganhowarth.com

Jeff Kroeze Photography
Orange County, California
949-633-5966
www.jeffkroeze.com

Thomas McConnell
Austin, Texas
512-426-8368
www.mcconnellphoto.net
www.starlightpictures.com

Charles Meachum
Malvern, Pennsylvania
www.charlesmeacham.com

Scott Moore Photography
Florida
404-312-8562
www.scottmoorephoto.com

Henry Nelson
Wichita, Kansas
316-683-7834
www.henrynelson.net

Eugene Parciasepe, Jr.
Wood-Ridge, New Jersey
973-214-0907
www.genophoto.com

Dustin Peck Photography
980-721-6290

Marisa Pellegrini Photography
646-296-7762
marisapellegrini.com

Diane Purcell, Through the Lens, Inc.
512-847-7506
www.ttlmgt.com

Jay Rosenblatt
Milburn, New Jersey
973-731-1616
www.jayrosenblatt.com

Bill Rothschild
Wesley Hills, New York
845-354-4567

Eric Schmidt
626-357-7712
www.ericschmidtphotography.com

Angie Seckinger
Potomac, Maryland
301-983-9846
www.angieseckinger.com/

Showcase by Agent
Franklin, Tennessee
615-301-3911

Ray Strawbridge
Bunn, North Carolina
919-496-3008
www.StrawbridgePhoto.com

David Van Scott Photography
Asbury, New Jersey
908-730-6174
www.vanscottphoto.com

Steven Paul Whitsitt Photography
Durham, North Carolina
919-624-7018